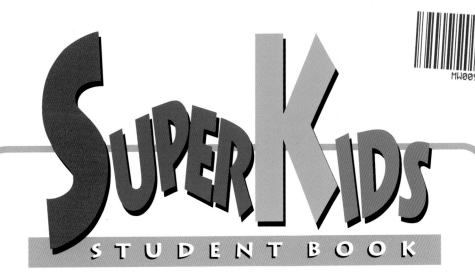

SuperKids
STUDENT BOOK

4

Aleda Krause
Greg Cossu

DON

BETH

KIM

CHIP

CHUCK

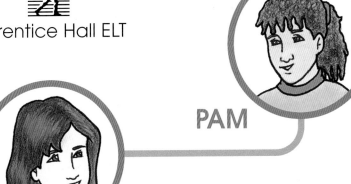

PAM

SANDY

Prentice Hall ELT

Acknowledgements:

The authors would like to express their sincere gratitude to Lesley Koustaff for her commitment and contribution to this project.

To my husband, my own ET: without his constant, loving support and assistance this book would never have been finished; and to my father, JP, who taught me to persist, in spite of any obstacles. Also to Setsuko: your input was always invaluable and uplifting; and to Yuri, for 'tweaking' things in the right direction. I'd like to thank Eriko, Atsuko and Yukiko for their on-the-mark comments. Finally, to Deborah, for helping me to the right path in the first place.

Aleda Krause

I would like to express my sincere thanks to our editors and advisors: Karen Jamieson, Nicola Miller, Setsuko Toyama and Yuri Kuno, my co-author, Aleda Krause and all of the marketing and support staff at Prentice Hall, my dear friends the Mizunos and Yoshita Kajimoto for all their day to day encouragement and Yoneo Nakamura who helped me get started in the field of EFL. I would like to dedicate SuperKids to my parents, my sister Pam and my brother David. Thanks for always being there.

Greg Cossu

Prentice Hall Asia would like to thank the following people for their invaluable input in the early stages of SuperKids: Noriko Campbell, Judith Evans, Lori Haga, David Haines, Etsuko Hayakawa, Katsuko Ichikawa, International Education Systems, Inc. staff and teachers, Reiko Kato, Hiromi Kikuchi, Aki Kizaki, Michiko Kunitomo, Rohit Nagji, Shoko Noguchi, Ray and Masumi Ormandy, Mieko Shinbo, Reiko Tada, Mitsue Tamai-Allen, Eiko Tsuchida, Masue Umehara, Shawna Wiggins, Eriko Yamakawa.

Publishing Director: Stephen Troth
Editorial Director: Marion Cooper
Publisher: Karen Jamieson
Managing Editor: Emanden Publishers / Nicola Miller
Development Editor: Setsuko Toyama
Series Adviser: Yuri Kuno
Production Manager: Oliver Lam
Design, Illustration, and Production: Marketing Horizons / Betty B. Bravo
Art Director: Caesar M. Velez
Illustrators: Michele Enriquez, Apol Geronimo, Gem Habito,
　　　　　　　Sonny Ramirez, Arnold Ramos
Colorists: Wowie Lopez, Michael Marcos, Tristan Garcia
Computer Graphics: Ivy Villamiel

First published 1998 by
Prentice Hall Asia ELT
317 Alexandra Road
#04-01 IKEA Building
Singapore 159965

©Prentice Hall Japan

Printed and bound in Singapore

ISBN 4-931356-78-8 SuperKids Student Book 4

5 4 3 2 1

Table of Contents

Syllabus

Unit	Title	Topics	Dialogs (*are substitution dialogs)
1	Last day of school	Countries Greetings Vacation actions	School's out in three days. Hooray! I can't wait. *Can we go to Australia? Sure. All right! *This is our guide, Mr. Gray. Good morning, Mr. Gray. Nice to meet you.
2	At the airport	Personal items Facilities Possessive pronouns	*Excuse me. Where's the restroom? Right over there. Thank you. *Oh, shoot! I forgot my handkerchief. Here. Use mine. Thanks a lot. What's your name? I'm Beth Green. How old are you? I'm 12.
3	Japan	Languages Buying things Numbers	*Do you speak English? Uh-huh. Do you speak Japanese? Yes. A little. *How much is this? It's 1000 yen. O.K. I'll take it. What time do we leave? At 6:30. Uh-oh. We have to hurry.
Recycle 1	Review of Units 1–3	Board Game	
4	Australia	Describing animals/winter Australian animals Animal food	*I like koalas. Why? They're soft. *I don't like winter. Why not? It's too cold. *What did you see? A kangaroo and a platypus. Awesome!
5	South Africa	South African Animals Feelings Comparisons	*Guess what! What? I see a hippo. Look at that! Wow! Take a picture! *This is fun, isn't it? Yeah.
6	England	Clothing Actions on a trip	Oh no! Chuck's lost. You're kidding. *What's he wearing? A blue sweatshirt and white shorts. *There he is! He's buying fish and chips. That's not fair!
Recycle 2	Review of Units 4–6	Board Game	
7	France	Fruit Cities Actions	*Where are you from? I'm from Paris. Oh, really. *What's this in English? A peach. Do you want one? No, thanks. Be careful. Watch your step. O.K. Help!!!
8	The U.S.	Occupations Ailments Picnic food	This place is great. Look! A roller coaster! Come on, guys! *I want to be an astronaut. Not me. I want to be a firefighter. *Are you O.K.? No. I have a stomachache. Why don't you sit down?
9	Back home again	Souvenirs Describing past events Countries	*How was the trip? It was fantastic! *Here's a souvenir for you. Thank you. It's a boomerang. Good night. Sleep tight. I missed you. Good night.
Recycle 3	Review of Units 7–9	Board Game	

Unit	Title	Topics
Culture 1	Happy Birthday	Birthday activities
Culture 2	Easter	Easter items
Culture 3	Christmas	Christmas items
Culture 4	More Holidays Around the World	Holiday activities

Kidioms	Vocabulary		Grammar	Phonics
Hooray! All right!	Australia Japan South Africa England France the U.S.	Good morning. Good afternoon. Good evening. Hello.	I'm/We're/They're going to *build a treehouse.* What are you/they going to do tonight? I'm/We're/ They're going to *study math.*	Review ay ai a_e
Oh, shoot!	restroom telephone restaurant gift shop	handkerchief comb soap toothpaste	It's/It's not *yours/mine/his/hers.* It's *mine.* Whose *suitcase* is this? It's ours/yours (pl.)/theirs.	Review oa ow o_e
Uh-huh. Uh-oh.	Japanese French Korean Chinese	10–100 100–1000	The *wallets* are behind/in front of/next to the *fans.* Where are the *postcards?* They're across from/ next to/behind/in front of the *mugs.*	Review ee ea Introduce ie
Awesome!	soft cuddly cold windy	a kangaroo a platypus a crocodile a penguin	She/He has some *fish.* Does she/he have any *leaves?* Yes, she/he does. / No, she/he doesn't.	ew oo u_e
Guess what! Wow!	a hippo a giraffe a leopard a rhino	fun scary exciting super	*A rhino* is bigger/smaller/faster/slower than *a hippo.* Is *a giraffe* taller/shorter/fatter/thinner than *a kangaroo?* Yes, it is. / No, it isn't.	oi oy
You're kidding. That's not fair!	a sweatshirt a dress shorts boots	fish and chips fried chicken pizza fruit	He/I was in *the toy store.* / We/They were in *the post office.* Where was she? She was in *the game center.* Where were you (sing.)? I was in *the game center.* Where were you (pl.)/they? We/They were in *the bookstore.*	ow ou
Oh, really.	Paris London Tokyo Sydney Cape Town Los Angeles	a peach a pear a tangerine a plum	He/She wants to *go swimming.* He/She doesn't want to *go shopping.* What does she/he want to do? She/He wants to *have lunch.*	ie igh y
Come on, guys!	an astronaut a firefighter a nurse a police officer	a stomachache a headache a toothache a cold	There's some *juice* in the basket. There are some *crackers* in the basket. Is there any *lemonade?* Yes, there is./No, there isn't. Are there any *cookies?* Yes, there are./No, there aren't.	ar or
Fantastic! Sleep tight.	trip movie picnic birthday party	a boomerang a poster a spoon a necktie	I/We/He/She *rode a roller coaster* in *the U.S.* What did you (sing. & pl.)/she/they do in *England?* I/We/She/They *ate fish and chips.*	ir er ur

Commentary

We swim and play games. We blow out candles and open birthday presents. We drink fruit juice. We have a birthday party. We eat cake and have a balloon relay. We eat birthday cake and ice cream. We play games, too.

We watch a parade and catch flowers. We dye eggs. We put the eggs in an Easter basket. We make Easter bunnies at school. We eat hot cross buns. We look for chocolate Easter eggs in the garden. We eat the eggs.

We pull Christmas crackers. We look for coins in the Christmas pudding. We hang Christmas lights outside. We sing Christmas carols. We light sparklers. We sing songs with our families. We have a picnic on the beach. We eat turkey and ham.

January 1 is New Year's Day. We wear kimonos and go to a shrine. We get New Year's money. July 4 is Independence Day in the U.S. We watch fireworks and have a picnic. May 5 is Children's Day. Boys make carp streamers. November 5 is Guy Fawkes Day. We make a bonfire and bake potatoes.

Talk about it!

Listen. Point.

Australia

Japan

South Africa

England

France

the U.S.

Good morning.

Good afternoon.

Good evening.

Hello.

Build it! 1

Vocabulary.
Listen. Repeat.

We   They

I

1

build a treehouse

2

take a trip

3

do a project

4

write a story

Listen. Repeat.

We're going to build a treehouse.

I'm	
We're	going to build a treehouse.
They're	

Practice.

1  .

2   .

3   .

4  .

5  .

6  .

I'm = I am   We're = We are   They're = They are

Build it! 2

Vocabulary.
Listen. Repeat.

you

you

they

1 study math

2 watch TV

I

We

3 read comic books

4 play soccer

tonight

Listen. Repeat.

What are you going to do tonight?

I'm going to study math.

What are you / they going to do tonight?

I'm
We're going to study math.
They're

Ask. Answer.

1 ?  .

2 ?  .

3 ?  .

4 ?  .

Sing-A-Gram. 🔲

Review it! 1

Listen. Number.

 # Use it!

Listen. Repeat.

 What are you going to do?   I'm going to write a story.

1. **A** is about you. Circle one each in 1,2,3 and 4.
2. **B** is about your partner. Ask questions. Circle your partner's answers in **B**.

A

1	watch TV	read comic books
2	play soccer	build a treehouse
3	read comic books	write a story
4	take a trip	study math

B

1	watch TV	read comic books
2	play soccer	build a treehouse
3	read comic books	write a story
4	take a trip	study math

Check: Does your **A** look like your partner's **B**?

 # My Choice!

Draw. Tell your partner.

I'm going to [   ] .

Read it!

Listen. Point.

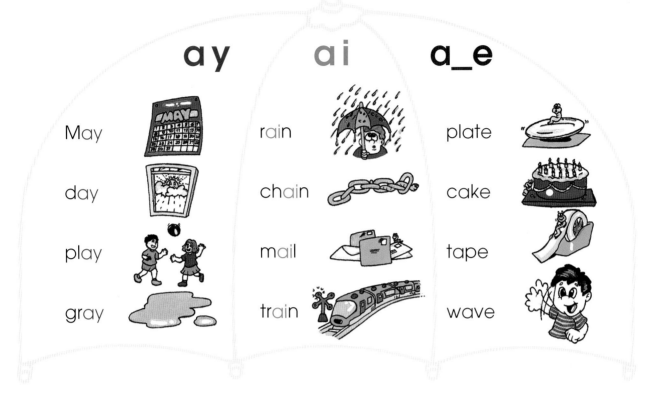

a y

May

day

play

gray

a i

rain

chain

mail

train

a_e

plate

cake

tape

wave

Match it!

Read. Match.

It's a gray day in May.

The cake is on the plate.

Wave to the mailman.

Play with a train.

Review it! 2

Listen. Check.

1
Australia | Japan

2
South Africa | France

3
Good afternoon. | Good evening.

4
play soccer | build a treehouse

5
cake on a plate | cake on a train

6
gray rain | gray tape

 # Chant it!

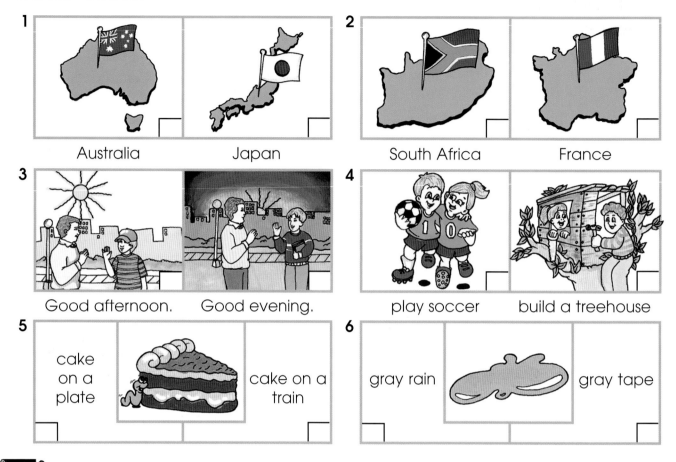

Good morning. Good morning.
This is Mr. Gray.
Nice to **meet** you, Mr. Gray.
Nice to meet **you**.

Hello. Hello.
This is Ms. Lee.
Nice to **meet** you, Ms. Lee.
Nice to meet **you**.

 Enjoy it!

It's a gray day in May.
Mr. Mouse is going to take a trip.

Are you ready, Mr. Mouse?

8

Talk about it!

Listen. Point.

restroom

telephone

restaurant

gift shop

handkerchief

comb

soap

toothpaste

Build it! 1

Vocabulary.
Listen. Repeat.

1
yours

2
mine

3
his

4
hers

Listen. Repeat.

It's not yours. It's mine.

		yours.
It's		mine.
It's not	his.
		hers.

Practice.

1 . .

2 . .

3 .

4 . .

5 . .

6 .

it's = it is

 **Build it! 2**

**Vocabulary.
Listen. Repeat.**

ours

yours

theirs

1
suitcase

2
camera

3
video camera

4
alarm clock

Listen. Repeat.

Whose suitcase is this?

It's ours.

Whose suitcase is this?

It's ours.
yours.
theirs.

Ask. Answer.

1  ? .

2  ? .

3  ? .

4  ? .

Sing-A-Gram.

12

Review it! 1

Listen. Number.

 # Use it!

Listen. Repeat.

Whose camera is this?
Whose suitcase is this?

It's his.
It's hers.

1. Look at **A**. Draw a line from each object to the boy or the girl.
2. Ask questions. Draw a line to your partner's answers in **B**.

A **B**

Check: Does your **A** look like your partner's **B**?

 # My Choice!

Draw. Ask your partner.

Whose  is this?

Read it!

Listen. Point.

o a	o w	o _ e
toast	snow	pole
soap	bowl	stone
goal	crow	phone
coach	throw	home

Match it!

Read. Match.

The toast is in a bowl.

Throw the stone to the coach.

The crow is on the goal.

a phone in a home

Review it! 2

Listen. Check.

1

restaurant   gift shop

2

restroom   telephone

3

handkerchief   comb

4

suitcase   camera

5

soap in a bowl   a stone in a bowl

6

a crow on a pole   a crow on a coach

Chant it!

What's your name?
I'm Ken.
How old are you?
I'm 10.

What's your name?
I'm Kate.
How old are you?
I'm 8.

What's your name?
I'm Kevin.
How old are you?
I'm 11.

 **Enjoy it!**

Mr. Mouse is at the airport.
Whose phone is that?

Don't be late, Mr. Mouse.

16

UNIT 3

Talk about it!

Listen. Point.

Japanese

French

Korean

Chinese

Mount Fuji

10   100

20   200

30   300

40   400

50   500

60   600

70   700

80   800

90   900

1000

Bullet Train

Build it! 1

Vocabulary.
Listen. Repeat.

 behind

 in front of

 next to

1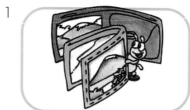
wallets

2
fans

3
pennants

4
T-shirts

Listen. Repeat.

The wallets are behind the fans.

	behind	
The wallets are	in front of	the fans.
	next to	

Practice.

1

2

3

4

5

6

19

 **Build it! 2**

Vocabulary.
Listen. Repeat.

 across from

 next to

 behind

 in front of

1
postcards

2
key chains

3
back scratchers

4
mugs

Listen. Repeat.

Where are the postcards?

They're across from the mugs.

Where are the postcards?

	across from	
They're	next to	the mugs.
	behind	
	in front of	

Ask. Answer.

1  ?  .

2  ?  .

3  ?  .

4  ?  .

Sing-A-Gram.   they're = they are   20

Review it! 1

Listen. Number.

 # Use it!

Listen. Repeat.

Where are the fans?

They're in front of the T-shirts.

1. **A** is your store. Draw one picture in each box.
2. **B** is your partner's store. Ask questions. Draw your partner's answers in **B**.

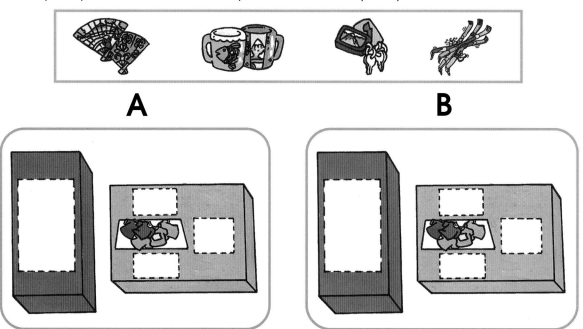

A

B

Check: Does your **A** look like your partner's **B**?

 # My Choice!

Draw. Tell your partner.

The [ ] are next to the [ ].

Read it!

Listen. Point.

e e	e a	i e
queen	peach	field
green	pea	piece
teeth	clean	handkerchief
sweet	eat	thief

Match it!

Read. Match.

The thief eats the sweet peach.

That queen has green teeth!

a green pea in a field

a piece of cake on a clean handkerchief

Sight Words

   has   of

22

Review it! 2

Listen. Check.

1

French | Chinese

2

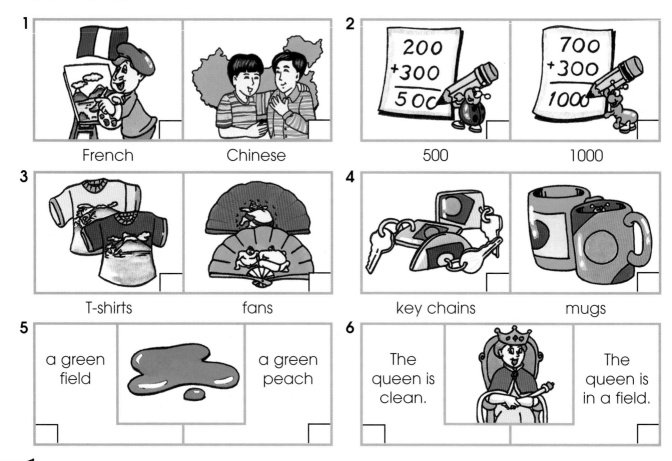

500 | 1000

3

T-shirts | fans

4

key chains | mugs

5

a green field | a green peach

6

The queen is clean. | The queen is in a field.

 # Sing it!

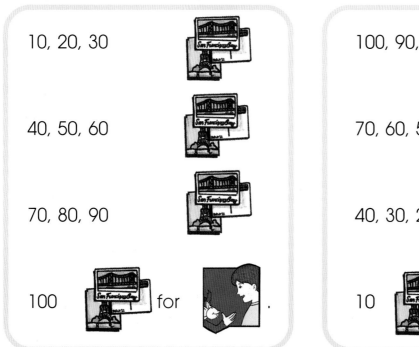

10, 20, 30

40, 50, 60

70, 80, 90

100 ... for ...

100, 90, 80

70, 60, 50

40, 30, 20

10 ... for ...

Mr. Mouse is in Japan.
His friend speaks English.
Don't forget to call Mrs. Mouse.

What's in the present?

24

Around the World

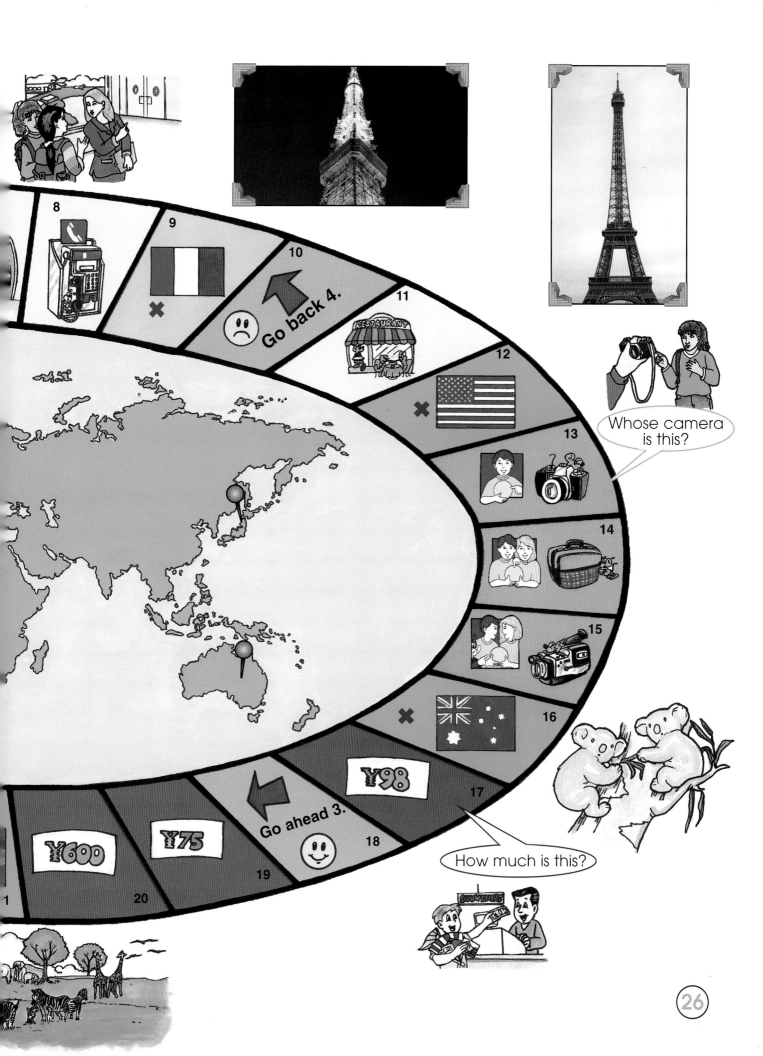

Talk about it!

Listen. Point.

soft

cuddly

cold

windy

Ayers Rock

a kangaroo

a platypus

a crocodile

a penguin

Great Barrier Reef

Awesome!

Build it! 1

Vocabulary.
Listen. Repeat.

She

He

1   fish

2   leaves

3   crabs

4   worms

Listen. Repeat.

She has some fish.

She has some fish.

Practice.

1  .

2  .

3  .

4  .

5  .

6  .

Build it! 2

Vocabulary.
Listen. Repeat.

she

he

1 leaves

2 fish

3 grass

4 shellfish

Listen. Repeat.

Does she have any grass?

Yes, she does.

Does she have any leaves?

No, she doesn't.

Does she have any leaves?
grass?

Yes, she does.

No, she doesn't.

Ask. Answer.

1   ? .

2   ? .

3   ? .

4  ? .

Sing-A-Gram.   doesn't = does not

30

Review it! 1

Listen. Write ✓ (Yes) or ✗ (No).

1  2  3  4

 # Use it!

Listen. Repeat.

Does she have any crabs?
Does he have any shellfish?

Yes, she does.

No, he doesn't.

1. Choose bucket **A** or **B**. Your partner chooses the other.
2. Draw 4 pictures from the box below in your bucket.
3. Ask questions. Draw your partner's answers in the other bucket.

Check: Do the buckets in your book look like the buckets in your partner's book?

 # My Choice!

Draw. Tell your partner.

She has some _____.

He has some _____.

Read it!

Listen. Point.

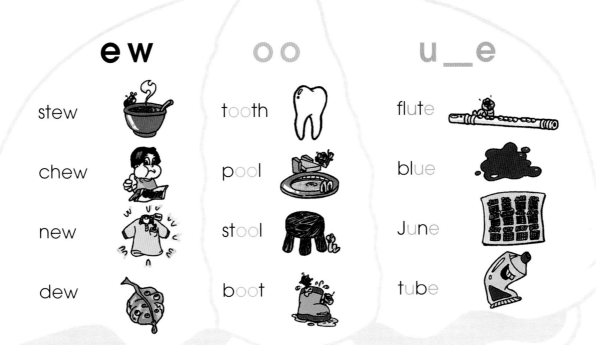

e w

stew

chew

new

dew

o o

tooth

pool

stool

boot

u _ e

flute

blue

June

tube

Match it!

Read. Match.

a new tooth in June

Chew the stew in the pool.

Play the blue flute.

dew on the boot

Review it! 2

Listen. Check.

1
cold   windy

2
worms   leaves

3
crabs   fish

4
kangaroo   penguin

5
a new flute   a blue flute

6
a tube in the boot   a tube in the stew

Sing it!

What did you see?
A ____ .
A ____ ?
A ____ .
What did you see?
A ____ and a ____ .

What did you see?
A ____ .
A ____ ?
A ____ .
What did you see?
A ____ and a ____ .

Enjoy it!

Mr. Mouse is in Australia.
It's June. It's winter and it's cold.
Watch out for the crocodile, Mr. Mouse!

What's in the present?

Talk about it!

Listen. Point.

a hippo

a giraffe

a leopard

a rhino

Table Mountain

fun

scary

exciting

super

Kruger Park

Build it! 1

Vocabulary.
Listen. Repeat.

big
bigger

small
smaller

fast
faster

slow
slower

1

a rhino

2

a hippo

3

a leopard

4

a crocodile

Listen. Repeat.

A rhino is bigger than a hippo.

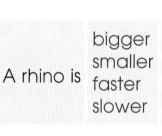

A rhino is | bigger / smaller / faster / slower | than a hippo.

Practice.

1

2

3

4

5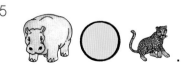

6

it's = it is

Build it! 2

**Vocabulary.
Listen. Repeat.**

tall
taller

short
shorter

fat
fatter

thin
thinner

1 a giraffe

2 a kangaroo

3 an elephant

4 a zebra

Listen. Repeat.

Is a giraffe taller than a kangaroo?

No, it isn't.

Yes, it is.

| Is a giraffe | taller shorter fatter thinner | than a kangaroo? |

Yes, it is.
No, it isn't.

Ask. Answer.

Sing-A-Gram. 🔊

38

Review it! 1

Listen. Write ✓ (Yes) or ✗ (No).

1	2	3	4

 # Use it!

Listen. Repeat.

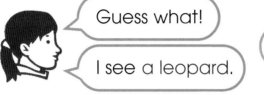

Guess what!

I see a leopard.

What?

1. **A** is your safari. Circle 4 animals.
2. **B** is your partner's safari. Talk to your partner. Circle your partner's answers in **B**.

A

B

Check: Does your **A** look like your partner's **B**?

 # My Choice!

Draw. Tell your partner.

I see a

Read it!

Listen. Point.

oi		oy	
coin		boy	
oil		toy	
boil		oysters	
point		soy bean	

Match it!

Read. Match.

The boy has a coin.

Boil the oil!

Eat oysters and a soy bean.

Point to the toy.

Sight Word

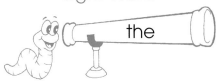

the

Review it! 2

Listen. Check.

1.
a leopard | an elephant

2.
a giraffe | a zebra

3.
tall | short

4.
super | scary

5.
Point to the toy. | | Point to the coin.

6.
oysters in oil | | a soy bean in oil

Chant it!

Guess what!
What?

I see a _____ .

Guess what!
What?

I see a _____ .

Guess what!
What?

I see a _____ .

Guess what!
What?

I see _____ .

Enjoy it!

Where is Mr. Mouse?
He's in South Africa.
Have fun, Mr. Mouse!

Guess what's in the present.

42

UNIT

6

Talk about it!

Listen. Point.

sweatshirt

dress

shorts

boots

43

Big Ben

fish and chips

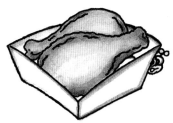

fried chicken

pizza

fruit

Stonehenge

Build it! 1

Vocabulary.
Listen. Repeat.

 He

 I

 We

They

1
the toy store

2
the post office

3
the bakery

4
the store

Listen. Repeat.

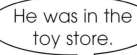

He was in the toy store.

We were in the post office.

| He I | was in the toy store. |
| We They | were in the post office. |

Practice.

1  .

2  .

3  .

4  .

5  .

6  .

Build it! 2

UNIT
6
46

Vocabulary.
Listen. Repeat.

 she

 you

 you

 they

 I

 We

1 the game center

2 the bookstore

3 the museum

4 the drugstore

Listen. Repeat.

Where was she?

Where were you?

She was in the game center.

We were in the bookstore.

Where was she?

I
She was in the game center.

Where were you?
they?

We
They were in the bookstore.

Ask. Answer.

1  ?  .

2  ?  .

3  ? .

4  ?  .

Sing-A-Gram.

(46)

Review it! 1

Listen. Write ✓ (Yes) or ✗ (No).

1    2    3    4

 # Use it!

Listen. Repeat.

  Where were you?   I was in the bookstore.

1. **A** is about you. Circle one each in 1,2,3 and 4.
2. **B** is about your partner. Ask questions. Circle your answers in **B**.

A   **B**

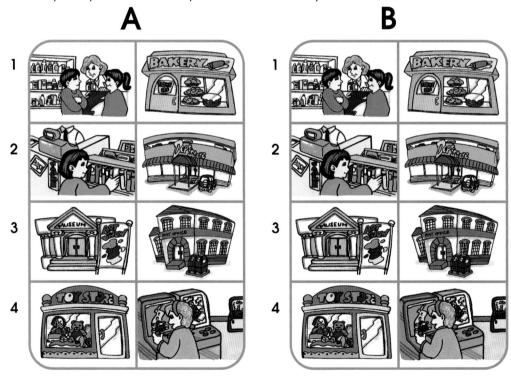

Check: Does your **A** look like your partner's **B**?

 # My Choice!

Draw. Tell your partner.

I was in the  .

Read it!

Listen. Point.

o w		**ou**	
clown		cloud	
brown		mouth	
owl		mouse	
cowboy		hound	

Match it!

Read. Match.

The cowboy has brown boots.

a hound on a cloud

The clown has a big mouth.

an owl and a mouse

48

Review it! 2

Listen. Check.

1

a sweatshirt   a dress

2

shorts   boots

3

fried chicken   pizza

4

toy store   museum

5

a clown and a cowboy   a clown and a mouse

6

a brown owl   a brown hound

Chant it!

What's wearing? What's wearing?

A and . A and .

What's wearing? What's wearing?

A and . A and .

You're kidding!

49

Enjoy it!

Now Mr. Mouse is in London.
There he is! He's on Big Ben.

What's in the present?
Here's a hint – what's the English mouse wearing?

Recycle it! 2

Up, Up and Away

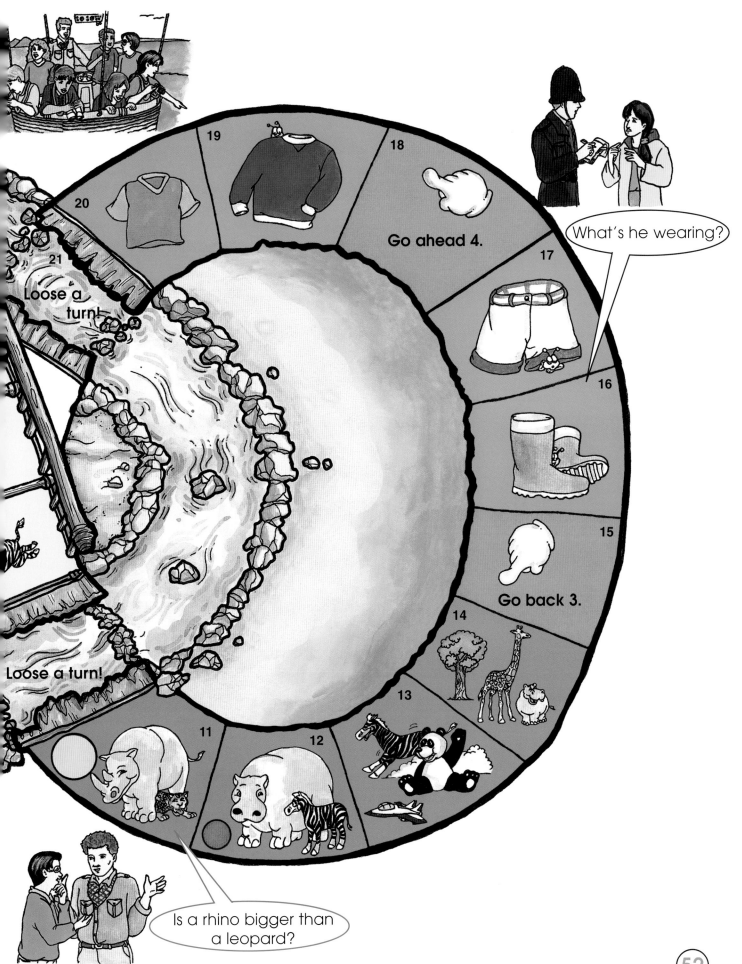

Talk about it!

Listen. Point.

Eiffel Tower
Paris

Tower Bridge
London

Tokyo Tower
Tokyo

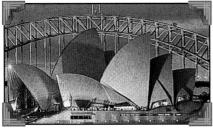

Sydney Opera House
Sydney

Cape Town

Disneyland
Los Angeles

a peach

a pear

a tangerine

a plum

Notre Dame

Build it! 1

Vocabulary.
Listen. Repeat.

He

She

1

go swimming

2

go shopping

3

have breakfast

4

go hiking

Listen. Repeat.

He wants to go swimming.

He doesn't want to go shopping.

He	wants to go swimming.
He	doesn't want to go shopping.

Practice.

1  .

2  .

3  .

4  .

5  .

6  .

doesn't = does not

 **Build it! 2**

**Vocabulary.
Listen. Repeat.**

she

he

1 have lunch

2 have dinner

3 go camping

4 play cards

Listen. Repeat.

What does she want to do?

She wants to have lunch.

What does she want to do?

She wants to have lunch.

Ask. Answer.

1 ?  .

2 ?  .

3 ?  .

4 ?  .

Sing-A-Gram.

Review it! 1

Listen. Write ✓ (Yes) or ✗ (No).

1  2 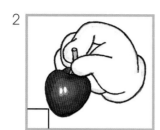 3  4

 # Use it!

Listen. Repeat.

What does he want to do?
What does she want to do?

He wants to play cards.
She wants to have lunch.

1. **A** is about you. Circle one each in 1,2,3 and 4.
2. **B** is about your partner. Ask questions. Circle your partner's answers in **B**.

A   **B**

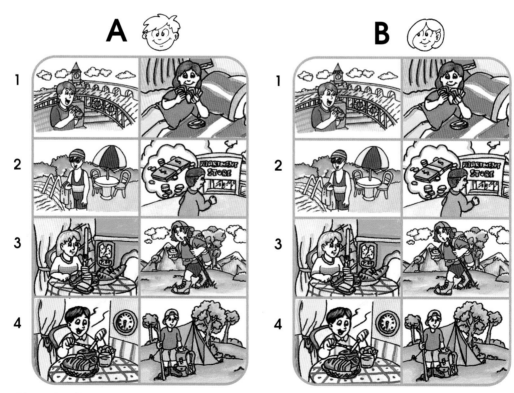

Check: Does your **A** look like your partner's **B**?

 # My Choice!

Draw. Tell your partner.

He wants to [   ].   She wants to [   ].

 # Read it!

Listen. Point.

ie

pie

necktie

spies

flies

igh

night

light

sigh

thigh

y

sky

my

spy

fly

 # Match it!

Read. Match.

She likes pie at night.

flies on my light

a spy on my thigh

Spies eat my pie.

Sight Word

she

Review it! 2

Listen. Check.

1
Tokyo   Los Angeles

2
a peach   a plum

3
a pear   a tangerine

4
go swimming   go hiking

5
a spy on my thigh   flies on my thigh

6
a light in the sky   a necktie in the sky

Chant it!

Where are you from? Where are you from?
I'm from Paris.
Oh, really!

Where are you from? Where are you from?
I'm from Sydney.
Oh, really!

Enjoy it!

Mr. Mouse is in Paris.
Oh no! There's a big bird.

Is the present a necktie?

60

UNIT 8

Talk about it!

Listen. Point.

an astronaut

a firefighter

a nurse

a police officer

Golden Gate Bridge

a stomachache

a headache

a toothache

a cold

Statue of Liberty

Come on, guys!

Build it! 1

Vocabulary.
Listen. Repeat.

1
juice

2
peanut butter

3
bread

4
crackers

5
grapes

6
potato chips

Listen. Repeat.

There's some juice in the basket.

There are some crackers in the basket.

There's some juice in the basket.

There are some crackers in the basket.

Practice.

1 .

2 .

3 .

4 .

5 .

6  .

There's = There is

 **Build it! 2**

**Vocabulary.
Listen. Repeat.**

1
lemonade

2
potato salad

3
chicken

4
cookies

5
sandwiches

6
raisins

Listen. Repeat.

Is there any lemonade?

Yes, there is.
No, there isn't.

Are there any cookies?

Yes, there are.
No, there aren't.

Ask. Answer.

1   .

2 ? .

3  .

4  .

Sing-A-Gram.   isn't = is not   aren't = are not

64

Review it! 1

Listen. Write ✓ (Yes) or ✗ (No).

1  2  3  4

 # Use it!

Listen. Repeat.

Are there any raisins?

Is there any juice?

Yes, there are.

No, there isn't.

1. **A** is your basket. Circle 2 food items. Cross out the others.
2. **B** is your partner's basket. Ask questions. Circle or cross out your partner's answers in

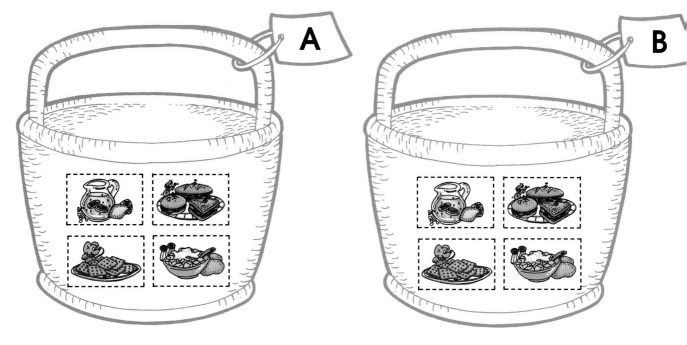

Check: Does your basket **A** look like your partner's basket **B**?

 # My Choice!

Draw. Tell your partner.

65

There's some [ ] in the basket.

There are some in the basket.

Read it!

Listen. Point.

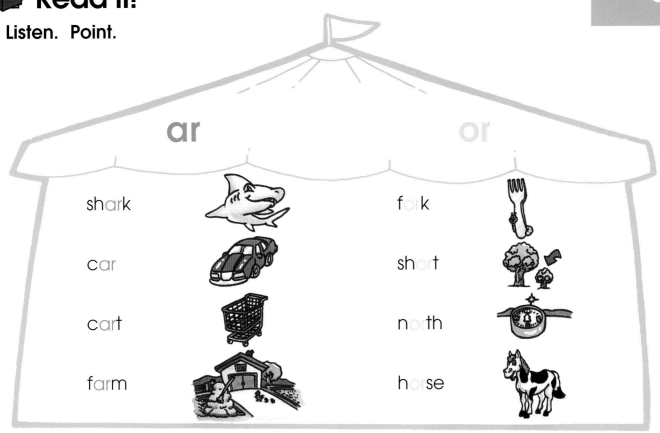

ar		or	
shark		fork	
car		short	
cart		north	
farm		horse	

Match it!

Read. Match.

The shark has a fork.

The horse drives a car.

a short tree in a cart

The farm is in the north.

Review it! 2

Listen. Check.

1.

a nurse   a police officer

2.
an astronaut   a firefighter

3.
a headache   a stomachache

4.
a toothache   a cold

5.
a farm car   a farm horse

6.
a short fork   a short shark

Sing it!

I want to be an .

I want to be an .

I want to be an .

Not me.
Not me.
Not me.

I want to be a .

I want to be a .

I want to be a .

I want to be a .

Not me.
Not me.
Not me.

I want to be a .

Enjoy it!

Mr. Mouse is in the U.S.
He wants to be a firefighter.
Have fun, Mr. Mouse.

What's in the present?

68

Talk about it!

Listen. Point.

trip

movie

picnic

birthday party

a boomerang

a poster

a spoon

a necktie

Build it! 1

Vocabulary.
Listen. Repeat.

I   we

he   she

1

ride a roller coaster
rode a roller coaster

2

speak French
spoke French

3

go to a museum
went to a museum

4

write postcards
wrote postcards

Listen. Repeat.

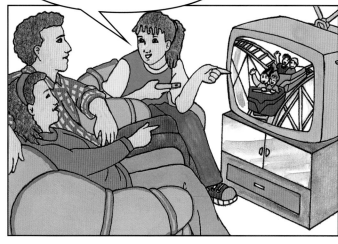

I rode a roller coaster in the U.S.

I rode a roller coaster in the U.S.

Practice.

1   .

2   .

3   .

4   .

5   .

6   .

doesn't = does not

Build it! 2

Vocabulary.
Listen. Repeat.

you

you

they

she

I

we

1
eat fish and chips
ate fish and chips

2
see zebras
saw zebras

3
take pictures
took pictures

4
buy souvenirs
bought souvenirs

Listen. Repeat.

What did you do in England?

I ate fish and chips.

What did you do in England?

I ate fish and chips.

Ask. Answer.

1 ?  .

2 ? .

3 ?  .

4  ?  .

Sing-A-Gram.

Review it! 1

Listen. Write ✓ (Yes) or ✗ (No).

1  2  3 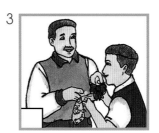 4

 # Use it!

Listen. Repeat.

 What did you do?) (I went to a museum.

1. **A** is about you. Circle one each in 1, 2, 3 and 4.
2. **B** is about your partner. Ask questions. Circle the answers in **B**.

A   B

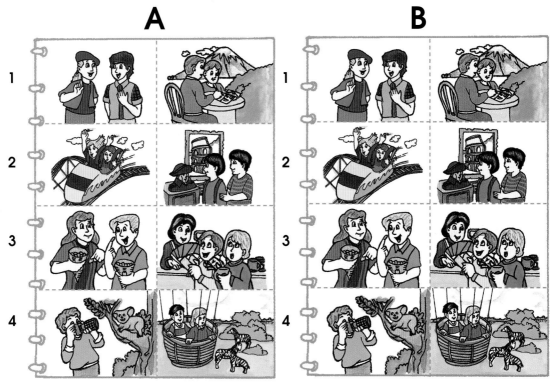

Check: Does your **A** look like your partner's **B**?

 # My Choice!

Draw. Tell your partner.   I  .

Read it!

Listen. Point.

i r		**er**		**ur**	
shirt		letter		nurse	
girl		sister		fur	
skirt		winter		purple	
thirty		teacher		turtle	

Match it!

Read. Match.

The turtle has a purple skirt.

a nurse in a fur shirt

a letter in winter

My teacher is thirty.

Review it! 2

Listen. Check.

1.

trip   picnic

2.

birthday party   movie

3.

a spoon   a boomerang

4.

a poster   a necktie

5.

a purple shirt   a purple turtle

6.

The nurse has a sister.   The nurse has a skirt.

Sing it!

How was the trip?

How was the trip?

It was fantastic.

Here's a souvenir for you.

Thank you.

You're welcome.

 **Enjoy it!**

Welcome home, Mr. Mouse.
Did you give your friends the letters?
What did you do?

International Kids

Listen. Point.

swim

have a
spoon race

have a
birthday party

have a
balloon relay

HAPPY

HAPPY BIRTHDAY

1

We swim and play games.

3

We have a birthday party. We
eat cake and have a balloon relay.

BIRTHDAY

We blow out candles and open birthday presents. We drink fruit juice.

We eat birthday cake and ice cream. We play games, too.

Let's sing!
H-A-P-P-Y
H-A-P-P-Y
H-A-P-P-Y
Happy birthday to you!

blow out candles

drink fruit juice

eat birthday cake

open presents

Listen. Point.

a parade

flowers

the Easter
bunny

hot cross
buns

We watch a parade and catch flowers.

We make Easter bunnies at school. We eat hot cross buns.

eggs

an Easter basket

chocolate Easter eggs

a garden

2 We dye eggs. We put the eggs in an Easter basket.

4 We look for chocolate Easter eggs in the garden. We eat the eggs.

82

Listen. Point.

Christmas crackers

Christmas pudding

coins

sparklers

CHRIS

1

We pull Christmas crackers. We look for coins in the Christmas pudding.

3

We light sparklers. We sing songs with our families.

83

Christmas
lights

Christmas
carols

turkey

ham

② We hang Christmas lights outside.
We sing Christmas carols.

④ We have a picnic on the beach.
We eat turkey and ham.

Listen. Point.

a kimono

a shrine

New Year's money

a carp streamer

AROUND THE WORLD

July 4 is Independence Day in the U.S. We watch fireworks and have a picnic.

November 5 is Guy Fawkes Day. We make a bonfire and bake potatoes.

watch fireworks

have a picnic

make a bonfire

bake potatoes

Picture it!

Unit 1

1

_____

2

_____

3

_____

4

_____

5

_____

6

_____

7

_____

8

_____

Unit 2

1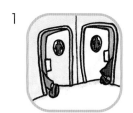

_____

2

_____

3

_____

4

_____

5

_____

6

_____

7

_____

8

_____

Unit 3

1  _____

2  _____

3  _____

4  _____

5  _____

6  _____

7  _____

8  _____

Unit 4

1  _____

2  _____

3  _____

4  _____

5  _____

6  _____

7  _____

8  _____

Unit 5

1  _____

2  _____

3  _____

4  _____

5

6

7

8

Unit 6

1

2

3

4

5

6

7

8

Unit 7

1

2

3

4

5

6

7

8

Unit 8

1
_____

2
_____

3
_____

4
_____

5
_____

6
_____

7
_____

8
_____

Unit 9

1
_____

2
_____

3
_____

4
_____

5
_____

6
_____

7
_____

8
_____

A
a 2
a little 17
across from 20
airport 16
alarm clock 12
all right 1
an 61
and 28
any 20
are 4
astronaut 61
at 18
ate 72
Australia 1
awesome 28

B
back scratchers 20
bakery 45
basket 63
be 16
behind 19
Big Ben 50
bigger 36
bird 60
birthday party 69
blue 43
bookstore 46
boomerang 69
boots 43
bought 72
bread 63
breakfast 55
build 3
bus 18
buy 72
buying 44

C
call 24
camera 12
camping 56
can/can't 1
Cape Town 53
cards 56
careful 60
chicken 64
Chinese 17
cold 27
comb 10
come on, guys 61
comic books 4
cookies 64
crabs 29

crackers 63
crocodile 28
cuddly 27

D
day 8
days 1
dear 34
did 28
dinner 56
do 3
does/doesn't 30
don't 16
dress 43
drugstore 46

E
eat 72
elephant 38
England 1
English 17
exciting 36
excuse me 9

F
fans 18
fantastic 69
faster 37
fatter 38
firefighter 61
fish 29
fish and chips 44
fly 60
for 24
forgot 9
France 1
French 17
fried chicken 44
friends 8
from 53
fruit 44
fun 36

G
game center 46
gift shop 9
giraffe 35
give 76
go 1
going 2
good afternoon 2
good evening 2
good morning 2
good night 70
grapes 63
grass 30
gray 8

great 61
guess what 35
guide 2

H
handkerchief 9
has 28
have 54
have to 18
he 29
headache 62
hello 2
help 60
here's 69
hers 11
hiking 55
hint 50
hippo 35
his 11
hooray 1
how 10
how much 17
hundred 18
hurry 18

I
I 1
in 1
in front of 19
is 2
isn't 36
it's 10

J
Japan 1
Japanese 17
juice 62
June 34

K
kangaroo 28
key chains 20
koalas 27
Korean 17

L
late 16
leaves 29
lemonade 64
leopard 35
letters 76
like 27
London 50
look 35
Los Angeles 53
lost 43
lunch 54

M
mail 8
math 4
meat 28
meet 2

mine 9
missed 70
mouse 8
movie 69
Mr. 2
Mrs. 24
mugs 18
museum 46
my 8

N
name 10
necktie 60
next to 18
nice 2
no thanks 53
not 10
not me 61
now 50
nurse 61

O
O.K. 17
oh no 43
oh really 53
oh shoot 9
old 10
one 53
our 2
ours 12
out 1
over 9

P
Paris 53
peach 53
peanut butter 63
pear 54
penguin 28
pennants 19
phone 16
picnic 69
picture 35
pizza 44
place 61
platypus 28
play 4
please 8
plum 54
police officer 61
post office 45
postcards 20
poster 70
potato chips 63
potato salad 64
present 24
project 3

R
raisins 64

read 4
ready 8
restaurant 9
restroom 9
rhino 35
ride 71
right 9
rode 70
roller coaster 61

S
sandwiches 64
saw 34
scary 36
school 1
see 28
she 29
shellfish 30
shopping 55
shorter 38
shorts 43
sit down 62
sleep tight 70
slower 37
smaller 37
soap 10
soccer 4
soft 27
some 28
South Africa 1
souvenir 69
speak 17
spoke 71
spoon 70
stomachache 62
store 44
story 3
study 4
suitcase 12
super 36
sure 1
sweatshirt 43
swimming 55
Sydney 53

T
take 2
taller 38
tangerine 54
telephone 9
than 36
thank you 9
that 35
that's not fair 44
the U.S. 1
theirs 12
there 9
they 3

thinner 38
this 2
three 1
time 18
to 1
today 34
Tokyo 53
tonight 4
too 27
took 72
toothache 62
toothpaste 10
toy store 45
treehouse 3
trip 2
T-shirts 19
TV 4

U
uh-huh 17
uh-oh 18
use 16

V
video camera 12

W
wait 1
wallets 19
wants 54
was 44
watch 4
watch out 34
we 1
wearing 43
welcome home 76
went 71
were 45
what 4
what's 10
where 9
white 43
whose 12
why 27
why not 27
windy 27
winter 27
worms 29
wow 35
write 3
wrote 71

Y
yeah 36
yen 17
you 2
your 10
you're kidding 43
yours 10

Z
zebra 38